A Day in the Life: Desert Animals

Gila Monster

Anita Ganeri

Heinemann
LIBRARY

Chicago, Illinois

www.heinemannraintree.com
Visit our website to find out
more information about
Heinemann-Raintree books.

To order:
☎ Phone 888-454-2279
🖥 Visit www.heinemannraintree.com
  to browse our catalog and order online.

© 2011 Heinemann Library
an imprint of Capstone Global Library, LLC
Chicago, Illinois

Edited by Daniel Nunn, Rebecca Rissman, and Sian Smith
Designed by Richard Parker
Picture research by Elizabeth Alexander
Production by Victoria Fitzgerald
Originated by Capstone Global Library Ltd
Printed and bound in China by South China Printing
 Company Ltd

14 13 12 11 10
10 9 8 7 6 5 4 3 2 1

**Library of Congress Cataloging-in-
Publication Data**
Ganeri, Anita, 1961–
  Gila monster / Anita Ganeri.
    p. cm. — (A day in the life. Desert animals)
  Includes bibliographical references and index.
  ISBN 978-1-4329-4772-9 (hc)
  ISBN 978-1-4329-4781-1 (pb)
1. Gila monster—Juvenile literature. I. Title.
  QL666.L247G36 2011
  597.95'952—dc22
  2010022820

Acknowledgments
The author and publisher are grateful to the following
for permission to reproduce copyright material: Alamy
pp. 7, 23 glossary desert (© Andrew Harrington), 8
(© Design Pics Inc.), 12 (© Roberto Nistri), 10 (© Rick &
Nora Bowers); Corbis pp. 17, 23 glossary poison
(© Kennan Ward); FLPA p. 14 (© ZSSD/Minden Pictures);
Getty Images pp. 16 (Barbara Jordan/Photographer's
Choice), 18, 21 (Jim Merli/Visuals Unlimited); © Jack
Goldfarb p. 22; Photolibrary pp. 4, 9, 20, 23 glossary
scales (John Cancalosi/age fotostock), 13 (Matt Meadows/
Peter Arnold Images), 11, 23 glossary burrow (C. Allan
Morgan/Peter Arnold Images), 15, 23 glossary predator
(Marty Cordano/OSF), 19 (PAUL FREED/Animals
Animals); Shutterstock pp. 5, 23 glossary reptile (© Susan
Flashman), 23 glossary insect (© Anke van Wyk), 23
glossary prey (© EcoPrint).

Front cover photograph of an adult Gila monster
(Heloderma suspectum) basking at the mouth of its den
reproduced with permission of Photolibrary (Wayne Lynch/
All Canada Photos).

Back cover photograph of (left) a Gila monster's scales
reproduced with permission of Photolibrary (John
Cancalosi/age fotostock); and (right) a Gila monster
somewhere in southwestern North America, reproduced
with permission of Corbis (© Kennan Ward).

We would like to thank Michael Bright for his assistance in
the preparation of this book.

Every effort has been made to contact copyright holders
of material reproduced in this book. Any omissions will
be rectified in subsequent printings if notice is given to
the publisher.

All the Internet addresses (URLs) given in this book were
valid at the time of going to press. However, due to the
dynamic nature of the Internet, some addresses may have
changed, or sites may have changed or ceased to exist
since publication. While the author and publisher regret
any inconvenience this may cause readers, no responsibility
for any such changes can be accepted by either the author
or the publisher.

Contents

Some words are shown in bold, **like this**.
You can find them in the glossary on page 23.

What Is a Gila Monster?

A Gila monster is a lizard.

You say the word "Gila" like "HEE-la."

crocodile

Gila monsters belong to a group of animals called **reptiles**.

Crocodiles and snakes are also reptiles.

Where Do Gila Monsters Live?

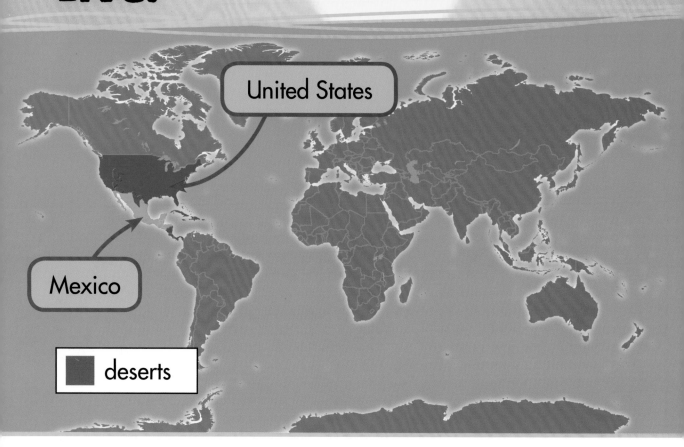

Gila monsters live in the **deserts** of the southwestern United States and northern Mexico.

Can you find these deserts on the map?

During the day, it is hot in the desert, but it gets cooler at night.

Gila monsters dig **burrows** in the sand or live in burrows dug by other animals.

What Do Gila Monsters Look Like?

Gila monsters have big, heavy bodies, with short, fat tails.

They can grow to be as long as your arm.

scale

A Gila monster's body is covered in black, pink, and yellow **scales**.

The scales look like small, round beads.

What Do Gila Monsters Do During the Day?

In the spring, the weather is cooler in the **desert**.

Gila monsters spend most of the day looking for food.

burrow

In the summer, it is very hot during the day.

Gila monsters stay in their **burrows**, to keep out of the sun.

What Do Gila Monsters Do at Night?

In the spring, Gila monsters spend the night resting in their **burrows**.

They come out in the morning to go hunting again.

In the summer, it is cooler in the **desert** at night.

Gila monsters come out at night to look for food.

What Do Gila Monsters Eat?

Gila monsters use smell to find their food, by flicking their tongues in and out.

They eat birds, eggs, mice, **insects**, and other lizards.

A Gila monster bites its **prey** with its powerful jaws to kill it.

Then the Gila monster swallows it whole.

How Do Gila Monsters Defend Themselves?

wild cat

If Gila monsters go out during the day or night, they have to watch out for **predators**.

Coyotes, hawks, dogs, and wild cats hunt Gila monsters.

If a predator comes close, the Gila monster opens its mouth and hisses.

Then it bites and chews its **poison** into its attacker.

Where Are Baby Gila Monsters Born?

egg

In the summer, the female digs a hole in the ground and lays her eggs in it.

She buries them and goes away.

The next spring, the eggs hatch and the babies crawl out.

They look like little adult Gila monsters and can already care for themselves.

What Do Gila Monsters Do in the Winter?

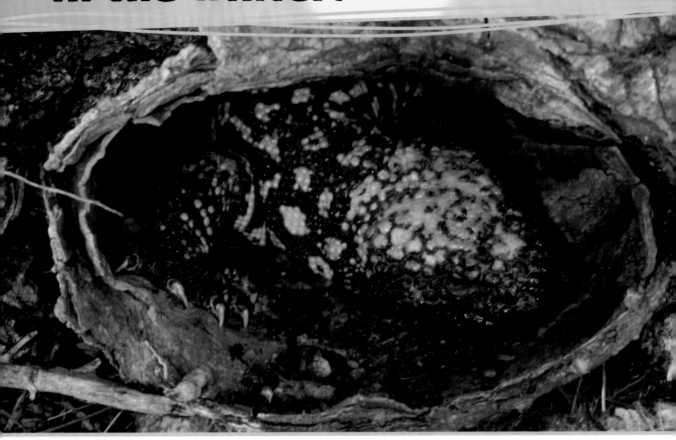

In the winter, it gets cold in the **desert**.

Gila monsters stay in their **burrows** and go into a deep sleep.

tail

The Gila monsters do not need to eat during the winter.

They live off fat stored in their tails until they wake up again the next spring.

Gila Monster Body Map

tongue

head

body

tail

eye

nostril

claws

leg

scales

Glossary

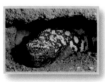 **burrow** hole in the ground where an animal lives

 **desert** very dry place that is rocky, stony, or sandy

 **insect** animal that has six legs, such as a grasshopper

 **poison** something that can cause illness or death

 **predator** animal that hunts other animals for food

 **prey** animal that is eaten by other animals

 **reptile** animal with scaly skin, such as a lizard or snake

 **scales** tiny flaps of hard skin on a reptile's body

Find Out More

Books

Haldane, Elizabeth. *Desert: Around the Clock with the Animals of the Desert* (24 Hours). New York: Dorling Kindersley, 2006.

Hodge, Deborah. *Desert Animals* (Who Lives Here?). Toronto: Kids Can Press, 2008.

MacAulay, Kelley, and Bobbie Kalman. *Desert Habitat* (Introducing Habitats). New York: Crabtree, 2008.

Websites

Learn more about Gila monsters at:
http://kids.yahoo.com/animals/reptiles/4420--Gila+Monster

Look at photos of Gila monsters and find out more about them at:
www.sandiegozoo.org/animalbytes/t-gila_monster.html

Index